MW01096743

How Our Government Works

35
J
328
Jak

What Does a GOVERNOR Do?

David J. Jakubiak

PowerKiDS press
New York

BCHS 26289
SCHOOL LIBRARY

For Bridget

Published in 2010 by The Rosen Publishing Group, Inc.
29 East 21st Street, New York, NY 10010

Copyright © 2010 by The Rosen Publishing Group, Inc.

All rights reserved. No part of this book may be reproduced in any form without permission in writing from the publisher, except by a reviewer.

First Edition

Editor: Amelie von Zumbusch
Book Design: Julio Gil
Photo Researcher: Jessica Gerweck

Photo Credits: Cover David McNew/Getty Images; p. 5 Bill Pugliano/Getty Images; pp. 6, 21 Shutterstock.com; p. 9 © AP Photo/Hans Pennink; p. 10 Joe Raedle/Getty Images; p. 13 Alex Wong/Getty Images for Meet the Press; p. 14 Streeter Lecka/Getty Images; p. 17 © AP Photo/Jim Cole; p. 18 Daniel Barry/Getty Images; p. 21 (inset) © AP Photo/Lauren Victoria Burke.

Library of Congress Cataloging-in-Publication Data

Jakubiak, David J.
What does a governor do? / David J. Jakubiak. — 1st ed.
p. cm. — (How our government works)
Includes index.
ISBN 978-1-4358-9358-0 (library binding) — ISBN 978-1-4358-9812-7 (pbk.) —
ISBN 978-1-4358-9813-4 (6-pack)
1. Governors—United States—Juvenile literature. 2. Governors—United States—Powers and duties—Juvenile literature. 3. U.S. states—Politics and government—Juvenile literature. I. Title.
JK2447.J45 2010
352.23'2130973—dc22

2009029405

Manufactured in the United States of America

CPSIA Compliance Information: Batch #WW10PK: For Further Information contact Rosen Publishing, New York, New York at 1-800-237-9932

CONTENTS

THE LEADER OF A STATE

When he ran for president in 2008, John McCain picked Alaska governor Sarah Palin to run as his vice president. Governors are often **candidates** for president or vice president. This is because they are proven leaders. A governor leads a state, just as the president leads the country.

Governors sit at the top of state government. They must understand the problems facing people in their state. If a storm strikes, a bridge needs to be fixed, or a bad sickness breaks out, people look to their governor. The governor and the people in the governor's office must be ready for anything.

Michigan governor Jennifer Granholm, seen here, worked closely with state and national leaders to save jobs in her state's car factories after hard times hit in 2009.

Some states require all children to wear bike helmets, but others do not. The age until which people must wear bike helmets is different from state to state, too.

STATE LAW AND FEDERAL LAW

On some New Mexico roads, people can drive cars 75 miles per hour (121 km/h). In Hawaii, the fastest people are supposed to drive is 60 miles per hour (97 km/h). States set their own speed limits.

As the federal government is, state governments are broken into three branches. One branch writes laws. One branch rules on laws. Governors lead the branch that carries out laws.

Some early Americans thought the country should have one set of laws. Others thought each state should rule itself. Instead, state governments and the **federal** government share powers. If a power is not given to the federal government, it is given to the states. State governments make their own laws about many things, such as hunting, fishing, and road safety.

A GOVERNOR'S POWER

Every state has laws that explain a governor's powers. These powers are different from state to state. In many states, the governor picks people to help govern the state. For example, every state has an attorney general in charge of **law enforcement**. In Alaska, Hawaii, New Hampshire, New Jersey, and Wyoming, the governor chooses the attorney general.

Some governors pick judges to sit on state courts, people to run state **colleges**, and groups that help pick people for other state jobs. In some states, the governor can even end the sentences of people wrongly put in prison.

In many states, lieutenant governors are second in command to governors. In 2009, New York governor David Paterson (right) named Richard Ravitch (left) lieutenant governor.

Governor Charlie Crist (right), of Florida, showed his interest in wildlife by helping scientists care for a manatee in April 2009. Manatees are large sea animals.

ANSWERING THE PEOPLE'S NEEDS

When a tornado ripped through Greensburg, Kansas, Governor Kathleen Sebelius ordered the **National Guard** to help the local people. As many states do, Kansas has laws that put the governor in charge of dealing with **emergencies**.

Even when there is no emergency, governors have many things with which to deal. They head up the state **agencies** in charge of helping people, nature, and schools. Governor Deval Patrick, of Massachusetts, helped scientists study bears to show his love of nature. On Thanksgiving, Governor Bob Riley, of Alabama, collected blankets for families in need.

WORKING WITH LAWMAKERS

In 2006, California governor Arnold Schwarzenegger signed a law to reduce the gases blamed for **global warming**. "We simply must do everything in our power to slow down global warming," he said.

Some bills are very long and include rules for many things. The governors of some states have a line-item veto. This lets governors veto certain parts of a bill.

The law began as a bill in the California State Assembly, a body that makes laws in California. Every state has a group of **lawmakers** who write and pass bills. If a governor signs a bill, it becomes a state law. Governors can also veto bills, or send them back to lawmakers. If enough lawmakers vote for a bill again, it will become a law.

Louisiana lawmakers passed a bill in 2009 that required that certain drunk drivers be sent to prison. Governor Bobby Jindal, seen here, signed the law that July.

In 2005, North Carolina governor Mike Easley (second from right) backed raising taxes to finance the NASCAR Hall of Fame, in Charlotte, North Carolina.

SPENDING TAX DOLLARS

In the spring of 2009, Governor Pat Quinn, of Illinois, asked state lawmakers to increase taxes. Without more money, he said, state workers would lose their jobs.

States raise money from taxes on things people buy and the money people earn. Things like license plates and speeding tickets also make the state money.

Most governors help decide how the state will spend tax money. For example, the money may be used to build schools or to pay police officers. In 30 states, only the governor can suggest a **budget**. In other states, this job is shared between the governor and the lawmakers. In most states, the governor's plan can be changed by lawmakers. Then, it is signed or vetoed by the governor.

RUNNING FOR GOVERNOR

In 1974, Ella Grasso ran for governor of Connecticut. Back then, the only women ever elected governor were the wives of former governors. Grasso was married to a school principal. She made history by winning the election.

Many states limit the time a governor can serve. In some states, governors can serve only two terms. Other states require a four-year break after serving two terms.

Voters in every state elect their governor. Most states hold **gubernatorial** elections every four years. New Hampshire and Vermont hold an election every two years. States generally require governors to be at least 30 years old. However, in California, Ohio, Rhode Island, South Dakota, Vermont, Washington, and Wisconsin governors need to be only 18!

Candidates for governor campaign, or try to get people to vote for them. Here, John Lynch (right) is campaigning for governor of New Hampshire.

The New York Governor's Mansion, in Albany, New York, looks out over the Hudson River. The house has been the home of the state's governor since 1875.

WHERE IS THE GOVERNOR?

On June 8, 2008, a fire ripped through the Texas Governor's Mansion. No one was hurt, but much of the building was destroyed. Texas governor Rick Perry worked hard to get the mansion rebuilt. The people of Texas even gave more than $3 million to help save this piece of Texas history!

Governors in almost every state have official homes in or near the state capital. Governors also spend lots of time in their state capitol. This building, which may also be called a statehouse, is the center of state government. It houses lawmakers and may also be home to the governor's office.

GREAT GOVERNORS OF THE PAST

Being governor has allowed different leaders to accomplish different aims. Governor Mario Cuomo helped New Yorkers go to college. New Jersey governor Christine Todd Whitman signed laws to help clean up her state's air and water. There have been many great governors. Before becoming president, Jimmy Carter, Ronald Reagan, Bill Clinton, and George W. Bush were all governors.

Wisconsin's governor Robert M. La Follette was one governor who was ahead of his time. While serving between 1901 and 1905, he chose women for top jobs in the state. This was even before women could vote! La Follette held a governors' meeting on **racial equality**, too.

La Follette (inset) pushed for big changes. In 1904, he won control of Wisconsin's Republican Party at a meeting in the University of Wisconsin Armory, seen here.

GOVERNORS GET TO WORK

Today, the governors of all 50 U.S. states are busy. The **issues** they face are great. Some governors are trying to keep schools and libraries open. Many governors want to bring more jobs to their states. Some are looking for ways to train workers to do new kinds of jobs. Still other governors are trying to make sure that all people can see a doctor when they get sick.

Think about the state where you live. What issues are important to you? What changes would make your state a better place in which to live? Take some time and find out what your governor is working on.

GLOSSARY

agencies (AY-jen-seez) Special departments of the government.

budget (BUH-jit) A plan to spend a certain amount of money in a period of time.

candidates (KAN-dih-dayts) People who run in an election.

colleges (KO-lij-ez) Schools people can go to after high school.

emergencies (ih-MUR-jin-seez) Events that happen in which quick help is needed.

federal (FEH-duh-rul) Having to do with the central government.

global warming (GLOH-bul WAWRM-ing) A gradual increase in how hot Earth is. It is caused by gases that are let out when people burn fuels such as gasoline.

gubernatorial (goo-ber-nuh-TOR-ee-ul) Having to do with governors.

issues (IH-shooz) Subjects with which people must deal.

law enforcement (LAW in-FOR-sment) Making sure that the laws get followed.

lawmakers (LAW-may-kurz) People who write and pass laws.

National Guard (NASH-nul GAHRD) A group of the U.S. military.

racial equality (RAY-shul ih-KWAH-luh-tee) Treating people of all races the same.

INDEX

WEB SITES

Due to the changing nature of Internet links, PowerKids Press has developed an online list of Web sites related to the subject of this book. This site is updated regularly. Please use this link to access the list:
www.powerkidslinks.com/hogw/gov/

DATE DUE

JA 1 5 '15			

DEMCO 38-296